Action Sports Library

Mountain Biking

Bob Italia

Published by Abdo & Daughters, 6535 Cecilia Circle, Edina, Minnesota 55439.

Library bound edition distributed by Rockbottom Books, Pentagon Tower, P.O. Box 36036, Minneapolis, Minnesota 55435.

Printed in the United States.

ISBN: 1-56239-074-0

Library of Congress Card Catalog Number: 91-073023

Cover Photos: ©ALLSPORT USA/PHOTOGRAPHER, 1991.
Inside Photos: ©ALLSPORT USA/PHOTOGRAPHER, 1991.

Warning: The series *Action Sports Library* is intended as entertainment for children. These sporting activities should never be attempted without the proper conditioning, training, instruction, supervision, and equipment.

Edited by Rosemary Wallner

CONTENTS

Mountain biking—an exciting new way to
explore the outdoors!

MOUNTAIN BIKING

What's a Mountain Bike?

A mountain bike is a strong, lightweight multi-speed bike. It has flat handlebars and very wide tires with rugged treads. A mountain bike can take a tremendous pounding—much more than the traditional and very common 10-speed bike. A mountain bike is designed to go where other bikes cannot go—especially in rough terrain. Yet it can still handle like a racing bike.

The mountain bike was developed from the BMX (Bicycle Motor Cross) bike. The BMX bike was designed for kids. It made its first appearance in the early 1970s. The BMX bike was small and very rugged. It could handle the rough terrain that a 10-speed bicycle could not. But the BMX bike had a major flaw. It had a very low gear. This made it difficult to use on the open road, steep slopes, and for long distances.

BMX bikes were used in California by kids to travel down rugged hillsides. They had so much fun that adults wanted to try it. But the BMX bike was too small for the adults. Even worse, once you reached the bottom of the hill, it was very hard to peddle to the top again because of the bike's low gear. How could kids and adults get more enjoyment out of this hillside fun?

Bicycle frame builder Joe Breeze got an idea. He duplicated the BMX design for an adult bike. Then he added more powerful handbrakes, a flat handlebar, and a gear derailer to help the rider climb hills. Suddenly, the mountain bike was born!

It took a few years before the mountain bike caught on with the public. The bikes looked very different from regular bikes. With their balloon tires and flat handlebars, many riders thought they looked funny. People were still used to the sleek design of the traditional 10-speed.

But slowly, people began to see how versatile the mountain bike could be. It worked well on the streets as a touring bike. And when you wanted to ride off-road, the mountain bike shined! People also admired the mountain bike's durability.

By 1983, several American and Japanese bicycle companies were offering their version of the mountain bike. Ten percent of all adult bicycle sales were mountain bikes. Even a mountain bike magazine, the *Fat-Tire Flyer,* appeared. By the late 1980s, mountain biking had become popular nationwide. An off-road cycling association was formed called NORBA (National Off-Road Bicycle Association). Today, mountain bikes can be found everywhere, from city streets to rural hillsides.

The Mountain Bike Up Close

The mountain bike's rugged frame is its most important feature. It is made of round tubular steel welded together at the joints. The frame is made up of the quadrilateral main frame, and the double rear triangle. The frame's length is greater than a 10-speed's frame. The space between the mountain bike frame and the wheels is also greater than in the 10-speed frame. This allows the mountain bike wheels to turn even when going through mud.

The fork of the mountain bike is thicker than the 10-speed's fork. This strengthens the fork, and allows the bike to withstand a

Mountain bikes have extra-wide tires.

greater pounding. The mountain bike has a flat and wide handlebar. This allows a more upright riding position for greater balance when traveling over rugged terrain.

The rugged balloon wheels are one of the most noticeable features of the mountain bike. They provide 90 percent of the cushioning. The tires can be over two inches wide (compared to the one-inch tires of a 10-speed). Even though they look slow, the tires perform just as smoothly as 10-speed tires. The key is proper air pressure. The rims of the tires are made of aluminum. They are wider and smaller in diameter than 10-speed rims.

As with 10-speed bikes, mountain bikes use derailing gears. The major difference between the two bikes is the amount of gears. Most mountain bikes come equipped with 15 or 18 gears. There are as many as three chainwheels and six back sprockets. This helps the mountain biker up the very steep hills. The pedals of the mountain bike do not have any toe-clips. Instead, the mountain bike pedals have large metal teeth for added gripping power.

Another special feature of the mountain bike is its brakes. Powerful brakes are needed if a mountain biker wants to tackle the steep hills safely. Cantilever brakes are used as opposed to the calliper brakes of the 10-speed. Only cantilever brakes work well on the balloon tires of the mountain bike. The brakes are operated by the levers that are mounted on the ends of the handle-bars. The brakes' cables are also thicker for added strength.

Even the mountain bike's seat is different. It is wider and offers more comfort than the 10-speed's racing seat. Most mountain bikes do not come with fenders. So if you don't want mud flying up your back and in your face, you'll have to order and install them yourself.

Taking Care of Your Mountain Bike

Just because the mountain bike was designed to take a pounding doesn't mean maintenance can be neglected. If you take care of your bike, it will last longer.

A mountain bike should be cleaned and lubricated after every muddy adventure. Don't let the mud dry. This can clog the sprockets and derailer. Hose down the bike and scrub the hard-to-reach places with a brush. When you're done, dry the bike. This will prevent rust. If the mud dries before you can clean the bike, brush it off first before you use the water hose.

Once your mountain bike is clean and dry, lubricate it. Use a spray can of thin-flowing lubricant like WD-40. Spray the derailing mechanism, the brake cables and levers, the chain, the chainwheels, the sprockets, and all joints and bolts. Be careful not to spray the sides of the wheel rims. This will make the brakes useless. If you do spray the sides of the rims, wipe them clean with a dry rag.

Choosing a Mountain Bike

Mountain bikes vary greatly in price (from $250 to over $3,000). Whichever bike you choose, most experts suggest that you buy your bike at a bicycle shop. This way, you are sure to buy a quality bike from a quality manufacturer.

Just because a mountain bike is expensive doesn't mean it is right for you. Choose one that's the right size. The best way to do this is to sit on the bike and test it for comfort. The balls of your feet should be able to touch the ground. If you're straining to touch the ground, the frame is too large for you. If your feet are flat on the ground and your knees are bent, the frame is probably too small.

When you grip the handlebars, your arms should be nearly extended, but your shoulders and hands should feel relaxed. If you're straining to reach the handlebars, the frame is probably too large. If you feel cramped, the frame is probably too small. Make sure you feel comfortable before you decide on a frame size.

Safe Mountain Biking

Mountain biking is more than just buying a bike and riding it. There are some safety tips that all bikers should know before tackling the hills.

Always be alert for other mountain bikers. Just because you're riding off-road doesn't mean you won't encounter other riders. Always keep your eyes forward and watch for approaching obstacles. Never attempt to ride down a hill unless you feel comfortable and in control. And when you're riding on the streets, watch out for cars. These rules may seem obvious, but riders often forget them.

Head injury is the most serious kind of biking accident. A serious head injury can lead to death. Experts recommend that all mountain bikers wear a safety helmet. The best kind of helmets have a fully enclosed plastic or fiberglass shell and are padded with foam. Avoid the sleek, attractive looking leather helmets that have openings. They may make you look good, but they don't give you much protection. Quality helmets can be found at any bicycle shop.

The more common injuries like cuts, scrapes, and bruises can be lessened if you wear the proper clothing. Long-sleeve shirts, riding jackets, and long pants made of a strong, lightweight material are recommended.

Don't wear anything that's too tight and restricts movement. Blue jeans may be comfortable in and around the house, but they can bind when riding a mountain bike. Never wear anything that might get caught in the bike mechanisms. Make sure your shoelaces are safely tucked inside your shoes. Tuck the end of your pant legs inside your socks. You may also want to wear riding gloves to protect your hands and improve your gripping power. Cycling clothes and gloves can be purchased at any bicycle shop.

How to Use the Gears

Mountain bikes come with 15 to 18 gears. Each is designed for the many types of terrain you will encounter during your mountain biking adventures.

The gears are shifted by the two thumb shifters located on the handlebars. Each shifter works its own derailer. There is a derailer for the back sprockets, and a derailer for the chainwheels. You must keep pedaling when you shift gears, otherwise the chain will not shift onto the next sprocket or chainwheel.

When riding on flat levels and smooth surfaces, select a middle gear. The lower gears are designed for various types of inclines, headwinds (when the wind is in your face), and road surfaces. Using a series of lower gears will give you smooth acceleration. Use a low gear when you want to

Know how to use the gears
before you tackle the hills.

accelerate quickly from a standing position, or when you find yourself riding in mud.

High gears are designed for downhill riding and for tailwinds (when the wind is at your back). Use a series of high gears to maintain a safe speed.

It takes practice to shift gears properly. The more you practice, the smoother the shifting will become. Try not to shift more than one gear at a time. And don't shift both derailers at the same time. Otherwise, the chain might come off.

Riding the Mountain Bike

Getting on and off a mountain bike is an important maneuver. It usually must be done quickly and often, and should not be taken lightly.

Stand on the left side of the bike. Make sure the left pedal is raised halfway up the chainwheel, and that the bike is in a low gear. Grab the handlebars with both hands and put your foot on the left pedal. Now swing the right leg over the seat and push down on the left pedal. As the bike moves, place your right foot on the other pedal—and start your adventure!

Paying attention to the way you get off your mountain bike is just as important as getting on. Place the bike in a low gear and slow down. When you've stopped, move forward from the seat so you are straddling the top tube of the frame. Now swing your right leg over the seat, maintaining a grip on the handlebars.

There are times when you will find it necessary to carry your mountain bike—especially around or over obstacles. Slip your right arm under the top tube all the way to your shoulder. Now grab the handlebars with your right hand and lift the top tube of the bike with your

The proper way to carry your mountain bike.

shoulder. Use your free left hand for balance or to push away obstacles.

Turning a mountain bike involves more than turning the handlebars. You also have to lean in the direction of the turn. The faster you travel, the more you will have to lean. You also need to lean when making sharp turns.

Braking techniques are also important for safe mountain biking. Usually, the left-hand lever controls the front brake. Use the front brake when making normal stops. When braking on a downhill slope, use both brakes. When braking hard, try to keep your body low and your weight back. This will prevent the rear wheel from rising off the ground— and causing you to tumble! As with shifting, practicing your breaking is a good idea. It will give you a better feel for your mountain bike, and more confidence.

There are three basic maneuvers that all mountain bikers should learn: 1) diverting, 2) log-hopping, and 3) ditch crossing.

Use the diverting maneuver to avoid hitting obstacles. First, briefly steer the bike *in the direction of* the obstacle. (This may seem odd, but it causes the biker to lean in the proper direction for a sharp maneuver.) Now quickly steer the bike *around* the obstacle, leaning the opposite way. Once your have avoided disaster, maintain your proper course.

Log-hopping allows you to lift your mountain bike over an obstacle. To log-hop, lean back and accelerate while lifting the front wheel over the obstacle. When the back wheel is about to strike the obstacle, lift yourself from the seat and throw your weight forward. This will allow the back wheel to bounce over the obstacle and lessen the chance for damage.

Ditch crossing allows you to do just that—cross a ditch. Ride into the ditch at an angle—and don't brake. Keep your weight back and stay low. When coming out, lift yourself from the seat and place your weight forward. The more your practice your maneuvers, the more confident you will become.

Places to Go

Mountain bikes are designed to take you anywhere. If you're just starting out and want to get to know your bike, try riding on smooth surfaces. Once you feel comfortable with your bike, you might be ready for some real fun on the off-road terrain.

You can go just about anywhere
on a mountain bike.

Downhill biking is the most exciting. For safety reasons, you should always go downhill biking with a group of bikers. If an accident occurs, you will have someone to help you.

Always wait your turn at the top of the hill. Don't ride down the hill together because you run the risk of collision. And never attempt a downhill run unless you feel comfortable and confident.

If downhill biking isn't for you, you might want to try cross-country cycling. Any open field will do. Be respectful of property signs and fences. There are many government-owned parks, forests, and preserves where a mountain biker can enjoy cross-country touring. Some even have horse trails that make excellent bike paths. Stay off of walking paths, however. Always be courteous of those on foot.

Competitive Mountain Biking

Since the formation of NORBA in 1983, off-road mountain bike racing has spread nationwide. One of the most popular events is the National Mountain Bike Championships. It is broken into two groups: juniors (adolescents) and seniors (adults).

Mountain bike racing is made up of many different events. In one event, a biker must cycle 20 laps around an obstacle course. In the uphill/downhill event, bikers must make their way to the top of a steep hill, then race down a marked trail. Times are kept for both the uphill and downhill parts of the event.

There is also an event called the Mountain Bike Challenge. This is a longer race that allows bikers to choose their own routes—usually through rough terrain. An even longer event is called the Enduro. Mountain

Competitive mountain biking
is growing in popularity.

bikers must do 20 laps around a two-mile obstacle course that contains all types of hazards, obstacles, and terrain.

If you think you're ready for any of these mountain bike events, contact one of the following organizations. They will inform you about upcoming races in your area.

NORBA
P.O. Box 5513
Mill Valley, CA 94942

LAW (League of American Wheelmen)
P.O. Box 988
Baltimore, MD 21203

Bikecentennial
P.O. Box 8303
Missoula, MT 59807

A Final Word

Mountain biking is an exciting way to enjoy the outdoors. Always exercise caution and courtesy, and you will make the sport safe and rewarding for all your fellow bikers.

GLOSSARY

- Cantilever brakes—brakes that use hinged levers to produce powerful braking.

- Chainwheels—the metal wheels turned by the pedals that move the bike chain.

- Fork—the part of the frame that holds the front tire.

- Gear derailer—the mechanism that moves the chain from one sprocket to another.

- Quadrilateral main frame—the main part of the bike frame, made of rounded tubular steel.

- Sprokets—a set of cog wheels that make up the gears.

- Treads—the grooved face of the rubber tire.

Visit the
LINCOLN
MEMORIAL

By Audrey Erin

Gareth Stevens
Publishing

Please visit our website, www.garethstevens.com. For a free color catalog of all our high-quality books, call toll free 1-800-542-2595 or fax 1-877-542-2596.

Library of Congress Cataloging-in-Publication Data

Erin, Audrey.
Visit the Lincoln Memorial / Audrey Erin.
    p. cm. — (Landmarks of liberty)
Includes index.
ISBN 978-1-4339-6398-8 (pbk.)
ISBN 978-1-4339-6399-5 (6-pack)
ISBN 978-1-4339-6396-4 (library binding)
1. Lincoln Memorial (Washington, D.C.)—Juvenile literature. 2. Lincoln, Abraham, 1809-1865—Monuments—Washington (D.C.)—Juvenile literature. 3. Washington (D.C.)—Buildings, structures, etc.—Juvenile literature. I. Title.
F203.4.L73E75 2012
975.3—dc23

2011031100

First Edition

Published in 2012 by
Gareth Stevens Publishing
111 East 14th Street, Suite 349
New York, NY 10003

Designer: Andrea Davison-Bartolotta
Editor: Therese Shea

Photo credits: Cover, p. 1, back cover (all), (pp. 2-3, 21, 22-23, 24 flag background), (pp. 4-21 corkboard background), pp. 5, 15 (main image), 17 (main image), 19, 21 Shutterstock.com; p. 7 Kean Collection/Getty Images; p. 9 (all) MPI/Getty Images; p. 11 Brendan Smialowski/Getty Images; p. 13 Panoramic Images/Getty Images; p. 15 (inset) Buyenlarge/Getty Images; p. 17 (inset) Sean Gallup/Getty Images; p. 18 Wikimedia Commons; p. 20 AFP/Getty Images.

Printed in the United States of America

CPSIA compliance information: Batch #CW12GS: For further information contact Gareth Stevens, New York, New York at 1-800-542-2595.

Contents

Words in the glossary appear in **bold** type the first time they are used in the text.

President of the People

Few presidents have truly lived the American dream. Abraham Lincoln did. He grew up in a poor family on the American **frontier**. Yet he made himself a success. Lincoln became the US president who guided the nation through a terrible time in its history—the American Civil War.

After his death, Lincoln seemed larger than life. It's fitting that his **memorial** in Washington, DC, displays him much larger than he was. Millions of people honor his memory each year by visiting the Lincoln Memorial.

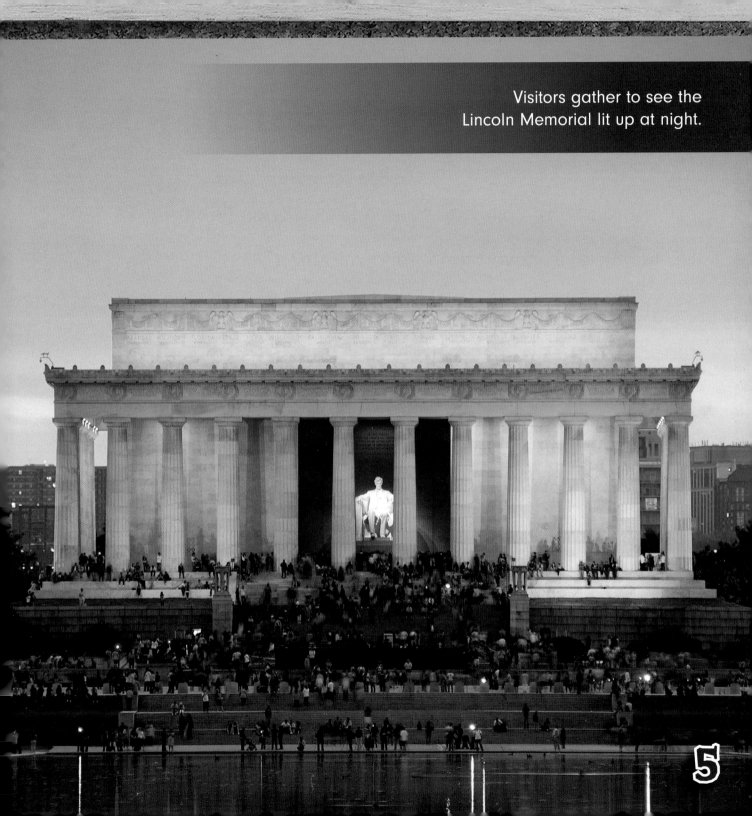

Visitors gather to see the Lincoln Memorial lit up at night.

Lifelong Learner

Abraham Lincoln was born in Kentucky on February 12, 1809. His family later moved to Indiana and then Illinois. He rarely went to school. He had to stay home to work. His mother taught him to read. People who knew Lincoln said he was always reading.

Lincoln became a lawyer and then served in the Illinois **legislature**. He ran for the US Senate in 1858. Though he didn't win, people respected him. He was asked to run for president in 1860.

Tell Me More!

Lincoln and his wife, Mary Todd, had four children. Only one, Robert Todd Lincoln, lived to become an adult.

Lincoln's childhood friend said Lincoln loved arguing his point of view with other children. This skill helped him fight Stephen Douglas (right) for a Senate seat in 1858.

The American Civil War

Lincoln ran for president as a member of the Republican Party, which was founded by an antislavery group. When Lincoln won the presidency, states in favor of slavery named themselves a new country: the Confederate States of America. The Civil War began April 12, 1861.

Many lives were lost throughout the war. In 1863, Lincoln freed slaves of Confederate states with the **Emancipation Proclamation**. In April 1865, the war ended with a **Union** victory. Slavery officially ended in the entire United States a few months later.

In a speech called the Gettysburg **Address**, Lincoln said that the goal of the Civil War was "that government of the people, by the people, for the people, shall not **perish** from the earth."

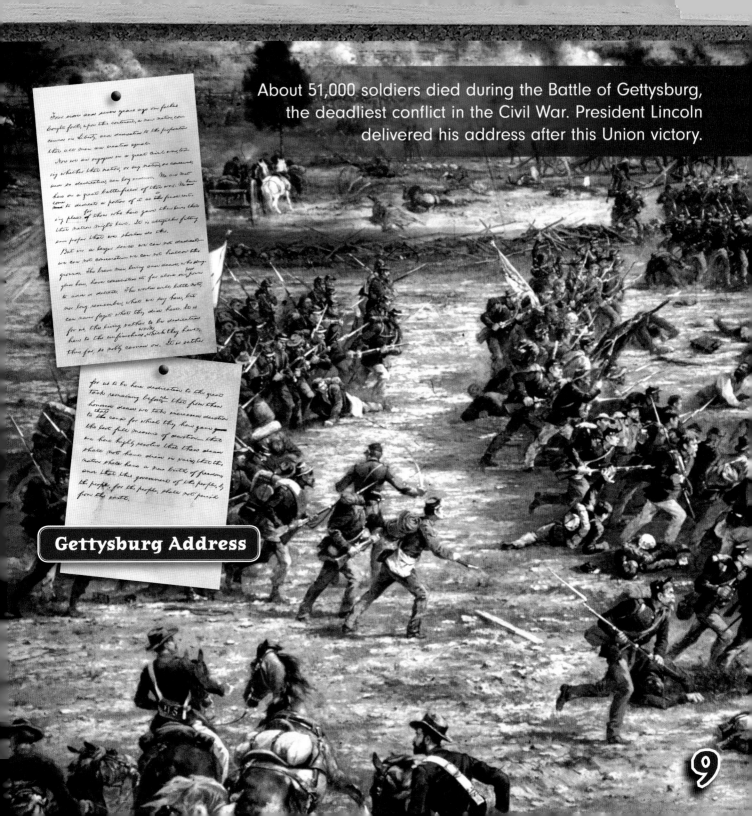

About 51,000 soldiers died during the Battle of Gettysburg, the deadliest conflict in the Civil War. President Lincoln delivered his address after this Union victory.

Gettysburg Address

Lincoln's Death

Just days after the Civil War ended, Lincoln was shot while watching a play in Washington, DC. He died the following day, April 15, 1865. Lincoln became a hero after his death. People realized how hard he had worked for his country.

To remember the man who saved the nation, monuments and memorials were created across the country. Two Lincoln statues were **sculpted** and placed in Washington, DC. But many thought this wasn't enough. They wanted a larger memorial.

This statue of Lincoln was created by 17-year-old Vinnie Ream. She was the first woman hired by the US government to sculpt a statue.

First Ideas

In 1867, Congress created a group to plan a large memorial for Lincoln. The first idea was to build a giant monument with many levels. At the top would sit the figure of Lincoln signing the Emancipation Proclamation. However, work never began.

In 1900, a new park system was planned for Washington, DC. It was decided that a memorial to Lincoln would mark the end of a park called the National Mall. The Mall is a strip of land that connects the Potomac River to the US Capitol building.

Tell Me More!

Another idea for a memorial to Lincoln was to build a road from Gettysburg, Pennsylvania, to Washington, DC.

The National Mall is pictured below with the US Capitol in the foreground. The Washington Monument stands between the Capitol and the Lincoln Memorial.

13

Bridging the North and South

The Lincoln Memorial location is on the Potomac River, across from Arlington, Virginia. This river had been a dividing line between Union and Confederate forces during the Civil War. The planners of the memorial saw this spot as a **symbol** of how Lincoln brought the two sides back together.

Congress formed another group in 1911 to watch over the memorial's construction. Henry Bacon was chosen to plan how the building would look. Work took place between 1914 and 1922.

Tell Me More!

Stones from Massachusetts, Indiana, Colorado, Tennessee, Georgia, and Alabama were chosen to build Lincoln's memorial. Together they're a symbol of a country united, thanks to Lincoln.

The Arlington Memorial Bridge connects Washington, DC, to Virginia. The Lincoln Memorial is shown at the foot of the bridge.

Lincoln Memorial construction

Stepping Inside

The memorial was made to look like a famous building in Greece called the Parthenon. Thirty-six **columns** support the structure, one for each state of the Union at the time of Lincoln's death. A state's name is written above each column.

There are three rooms, or chambers, within the building. The middle chamber houses a statue of Lincoln. The other two chambers display two speeches made by Lincoln: the Gettysburg Address and his Second **Inaugural** Address. Above each is a painting of an angel.

Tell Me More!

An "Angel of Truth" is shown standing with freed slaves in one painting in the Lincoln Memorial. It stands with lawmakers of the North and South in the other painting.

Parthenon

The photo below offers a view into the north chamber, which displays the words of the Second Inaugural Address. In this speech, Lincoln welcomed the Confederate states back into the Union.

E PEOPLE
E UNION
LINCOLN
ER

The Statue of Lincoln

Daniel Chester French studied Lincoln before sculpting him for the memorial. He wanted to show Lincoln's kindness and strength most of all. French sculpted the president's hands in a special way. One of Lincoln's hands is closed in a fist, showing his strength. The other hand is more open, showing his kindness.

Lincoln showed both kindness and strength in his leadership. He was strong when fighting to unite the country. Once the war was over, he offered kindness and forgiveness to the Confederate states.

Mathew Brady photograph of Lincoln

Daniel Chester French studied photos of Lincoln taken by famous Civil War photographer Mathew Brady before he began sculpting.

19

Memorial of Civil Rights

If you visit the Lincoln Memorial today, you'll also visit a special place in the fight for **civil rights**. On August 28, 1963, Martin Luther King Jr. gave a famous speech at the Lincoln Memorial. "I have a dream," he said. His dream was that whites and blacks could live together in peace and equality.

The Lincoln Memorial was a perfect place for King's speech. Lincoln had worked to free slaves. He had dreamed of peace, too. Lincoln will continue to be an example for heroes like King in years to come.

Martin Luther King Jr.

More Facts About the Lincoln Memorial

There are 58 steps from outside the memorial to the foot of the statue.

In the Second Inaugural Address on the wall, the word "FUTURE" was first spelled "EUTURE." The letter was later filled in to correct the mistake.

A mirror image of the memorial can be seen in the Reflecting Pool on the National Mall.

Lincoln's head looks down so that he appears to be looking at those looking up at him.

About 50,000 people attended the opening event for the Lincoln Memorial in 1922.

Glossary

address: a formal speech

civil rights: the freedoms granted to us by law

column: a tall, strong supporting post

Emancipation Proclamation: the announcement given by President Abraham Lincoln on January 1, 1863, that gave freedom to slaves in states opposing the Union in the Civil War

frontier: a part of a country that has been newly opened for settlement

inaugural: having to do with a beginning event, as in the inauguration of a president's term

legislature: a lawmaking body

memorial: a place, display, or event that serves as a way to remember a person or event

perish: to come to an end

sculpt: to create a shape with stone, wood, metal, or other matter

symbol: something that stands for something else

Union: the side of the Northern states in the American Civil War

For More Information

Books

Firestone, Mary. *The Lincoln Memorial*. Minneapolis, MN: Picture Window Books, 2008.

Hankins, Chelsey. *Lincoln Memorial*. New York, NY: Chelsea Clubhouse, 2010.

Rappaport, Doreen. *Abe's Honest Words: The Life of Abraham Lincoln*. New York, NY: Hyperion Books for Children, 2008.

Websites

Lincoln Memorial
www.nps.gov/linc/
This is the official website of the Lincoln Memorial and the best place to go when planning a visit.

Statues and Memorials: The Lincoln Memorial
bensguide.gpo.gov/3-5/symbols/lincoln.html
Read more facts about President Lincoln and his monument.

Index